MW01181624

EXPERT PROFILES
VOLUME 14

Conversations with Influencers & Innovators

EXPERT PROFILES
VOLUME 14

Conversations with Influencers & Innovators

Featuring

Karissa Adkins

with

Leslie Purdy

Arlea Hoffman

Barbara Beckley

Katie Bruno

Dan Obusek

Royalties from the Retail Sales of "Expert Profiles" are donated to Global Autism Project

Global Autism Project 501(c)3, is a nonprofit organization which provides training to local individuals in evidence-based practices for individuals with autism.

Global Autism Project believes that every child has the ability to learn and their potential should not be limited by geographical bounds.

The Global Autism Project seeks to eliminate the disparity in service provision seen around the world by providing high-quality training to individuals providing services in their local community. This training is made sustainable through regular training trips and contiguous remote training.

You can learn more about Global Autism Project by visiting GlobalAutismProject.org.

Table of Contents

RECLAIM YOUR BEST LIFE

While going through her own mental and physical transformation, Karissa Adkins began helping others achieve health and life goals through teaching simple habit changes. After assisting several women in living healthier lives, word got out, and she was referred to others who needed to improve their mindset, health, and balance practices.

Karissa's passion for speaking and teaching others grew bigger and bigger as she began to share her personal life stories and experiences with local audiences. Her dream of becoming a powerhouse coach, speaker, and published author is now her reality, and she is living her best life. Karissa is a certified Life, Health, and Mindset Coach through Health Coach Institute, Certified Personal Trainer through NAFTA, Global Speaker, Radio show Host, Founder of 365DailyHustle and BossUp Babe Radio, and a Co-Author of "Women Who BossUp!"

Karissa has been featured on networks such as ABC, CBC, NBC, Marketwatch, and more. Karissa found herself frequently being approached by women who needed advice, accountability, and support in regard to life's biggest challenges. Karissa brings practical, real-world experience to her coaching, mentoring, and speaking engagements. This magical concoction of personal setbacks and achievements paired with high energy vibes enables her to connect so deeply with her clients and audiences and create inspiring and transformational talks.

Her journey involves a complete mental, emotional and physical transformation. Not only has Karissa ran 2 successful businesses and gone through an emotional divorce, but she also achieved a 90-pound weight loss, successfully learned how to manage an autoimmune disease, and learned how to practice self-love and acceptance. Karissa prides herself on being resilient and helping her clients and audience navigate big life changes to achieve the lives they dream of. Karissa truly enjoys speaking and teaching women how to "BossUp" and rise above their current situation. Karissa helps purpose driven mamas lose weight, double their energy, and feel confident and sexy in their bodies.

Conversation with Karissa Adkins

What motivated you to become a health and wellness coach and advocate?

Karissa Adkins: My health journey has been much like a roller coaster with many highs and a lot of lows. Ten years ago, I weighed over 213 pounds. I'm five feet tall, so that put me in the obese category. I had a rock bottom moment. There I was sitting in the doctor's office, while I was stationed in Germany with my family. The doctor looked me straight in the eye and said, "Karissa, if you don't change your lifestyle habits TODAY, you might not be around for your daughter later on." Ouch, this was some hard to hear truth that made me sad, mad, and I was totally embarrassed.

I wasn't happy with my lifestyle and where my weight was; I knew my health was at risk. In that moment I was so upset with the doctor for being honest with me, but now I can see how here honest truth saved my life. Everyone tiptoes around the "overweight" subject, our spouses, our friends, and even our family members don't want to tell us the truth. Why? Because sometimes the truth hurts! That afternoon made me so mad that I went home and smoked a pack of cigarettes and drank a bottle of wine. I was so upset and frustrated not necessary with the doctor but more with myself. That night

I went to bed with the idea that tomorrow would be a new day, and that I would forget about the pain I felt from hearing the honest truth.

The next day I put my son on the bus for school and went to a friend's house, where I smoked half a pack of cigarettes and drank two pots of coffee. We sat, we talked, and we complained a lot about our lives. Later, I went home, sat on the couch and for the first time in my entire life I took a long hard look at the photo of my mother — all 320 pounds of her. I saw her battle cancer, diabetes, and the lack of energy she always felt. That day I saw myself in that picture. I heard my inner voice say, "Karissa you need to do something about your life, you need to raise your standards and get healthy, if not you are going to end up just like your mom!" Don't get me wrong, I love my mom. She was my best friend. She taught me so many major lessons in life. I just knew I wanted and needed to do something more for myself. That was the day that I BossedUp! I knew that in order to lose weight that I would need to get back to basics — I had to eat a little cleaner. I had to eat a little less. And I needed to start moving my body.

So, it started with that — I ate a little cleaner, ate a little less, and made it a point to move more. After about two weeks, I realized that this "new lifestyle" would be hard for me to keep up with by myself. So, I asked my neighbors to help me with support and accountability.

We started helping one another by exercising together and watching one another's kids so that we could work out.

My mother became my accountability partner. Why? Because she was the reason that I decided to BossUp in the first place. At first, my goal was to get under 200 pounds. In 2 months, I was able to see 198 on the scale, and I felt so happy when I made it to 190. Over time, my weight went down, and my confidence went up. It took more than three years to lose 90lbs but I did it, and I learned how to do it without dieting, excessive workouts, and guilt for motivation. Over the years, I started to talk to women about eating healthier and how to level up their workouts. By 2014, I weighed 145 and I felt amazing about my body, yet I still was not truly happy on the inside. I realized I would never be truly happy until I started loving myself for who I am first. So, what did I do? I invested in a coach and I started working on healing my trauma and loving myself. For the last five years, I have built some amazing habits that allow me to thrive in every area of my life.

I was moving forward, and in 2019 when I was diagnosed with Hashimoto's, which is an autoimmune Thyroid Disease that is incurable. So, how did I put Hashimoto's into remission without medication? I doubled down on my self-care, I eat clean food, I exercise, I sleep, and I learned how manage my stress. When my doctor sat with me and told me about the diagnosis, he said, "Karissa, thank goodness, you had that rock bottom moment 8 years ago and lost all that weight.

He said that if I hadn't changed my lifestyle and bad health habits, my symptoms would have been 10 times worse. I am thankful for all of the crappy and not so crappy moments that I have lived through, because without them I would not be here today! Today I have a new diet, a new lifestyle, and new things on which to focus on. Today, I can choose taking caring of me over everything and everyone else.

What motivates you to stay healthy?

Karissa Adkins: Being my best self is motivating to me. I made myself a promise 11 years ago; I'm never going back to 213! Over the years, I've built healthy habits and behaviors that I believe will help me never see that side of the scale again.

What motivates me is my why. Every man or woman trying to make big changes needs to figure out his/her why. 11 years ago, it was my mom and my kids, now beside them it's me 100%. Another part of my why is that I have a big purpose to fulfill; It's to inspire, motivate, and empower other women to invest in themselves and become healthy, happy, and thriving. I get to take what I have learned through personal experiences and setbacks and help other women accomplish their health goals. What took me 10 years to figure out I am teaching them in 10 weeks. When my clients BossUp, it inspires me to BossUp too. Every day I wake up and push myself to be the best version of me. Because when I am my best self-everyone else benefits too.

What tips do you have for women who want to start creating healthy habits?

Karissa Adkins: Building healthy habits is essential. First you need to understand your habits the good, bad, and the so-so ones, only then can you start to change them. Second, start changing and shifting just one habit at a time. A few of my non-negotiable habits are working out, getting my sleep, food prep, reading, mediating, and self-care. I built each of these habits one at a time.

You have many healthy habits. What does your average day look like?

Karissa Adkins: The cool thing about my workday is that it is always changing. However, there are parts of my day that are very structured. Which allows me to feel at piece and in control. My nighttime habits and routines allow me to get enough quality sleep which is crucial for me, because it sets up my morning routine. I wake up every single day at around 3:45 a.m., I'm off to the gym by 4:15. I work out from 4:30 to 5:30, then I go home and get ready for work. Part of my morning routine is eating a healthy breakfast, taking my supplements, making breakfast for my husband, and packing my daughter's lunch.

I have 30 minutes in my calendar scheduled every single day for my spiritual practice. This practice happens after I get back from school drop off, but before I "officially" start my workday. My spiritual practice looks a little different every day, but the time stays consistent. My spiritual time is spent mediating, journaling, or reading. This time is designated to me and getting my mind right and setting an intention for the day. I ask myself, "How do I want to show up today?" Since I have many client calls and speaking gigs, I give myself permission not to answer emails and I avoid social media before my spiritual practice. I like to do my gratitude practice during dinner which gets everyone around the table involved, even the guests.

Do you suggest diets or other nutrition to help create a healthy lifestyle?

Karissa Adkins: I don't believe in diets. It's important to think of food and nutrition as fuel and medicine for your body. Everyone should determine what type of food works for them. Personally, I choose a gluten-free, dairy-free, and egg-free diet. I found that I had sensitivities to those foods through allergy testing therefor I avoid them when possible. I believe that women need to ditch the crazy insane restrictive diets and become more intuitive eaters.

How do you juggle your family life, relationships, and business life? How do you find that balance in chaos?

Karissa Adkins: I think it comes down to knowing your priorities and knowing what's important to you. When I coach my clients, one of the first things we do is understand what is important to them. Life can get pretty crazy, pretty quickly if you let it.

If you are trying to figure out your big 5 priorities, ask the question: "If something was taken away from me today, what would I fight like crazy to get back tomorrow?" Everyone's priorities look different for various reasons. For me, my health and wellbeing is my biggest priority. My relationships are a priority; my business is a priority. My self-care "taking care of me" is a priority. My advice, figure out what's important to you, and everything else needs to become a "No."

Once you have your priorities identified, you can go from there. For example, after you have big five priorities in focus, ask what the next five priorities are that support your big five? Schedule everything by priority and know when to say, "No." Here is an illustration: If someone wants to hire me as the coach, but their goals are not health related, I kindly decline and refer them to another. Most people say they do not have enough time in the day to get it all done. I call that BS because I make the time for the things that are important to me. Second: schedule everything. I schedule my personal care along with my work schedule. It's color-coded, I schedule self-care, workouts, food prep—everything.

Priority scheduling is key to creating a healthy lifestyle without overwhelm.

If you were to itemize your keys to success for staying healthy and being in balance, what would they be?

Karissa Adkins: For me, the keys to success all come down to habits and mindset, creating healthy habits, and learning how to shift your mindset so that it works for you. One key to my success is exercise. There are so many benefits to exercise, not just physical, but internal —spiritually, mentally—exercise is just all around amazing for you.

What is one of the biggest lessons you learned about yourself as you reclaimed your health?

Karissa Adkins: My biggest lesson that I learned about losing weight and reclaiming my best life would have to be that I am worth it. 10 years ago, I didn't believe that I was worth investing in, I didn't feel like I was enough, I didn't feel like the queen that I do now. My intentions as a busy mama were always good. As a mom and a wife, I just wanted to take care of everyone else, I thought that was my biggest job. But looking back now, I ask myself what was I really teaching them? Not a whole lot. Through my transformation I have realized that I am not able to take care of everyone else if I don't take care of me first.

How important is it to have positive people in your life?

Karissa Adkins: So important! Remove toxic people from your life and to surround yourself with positive people you want to emulate. If you surround yourself with negative people who always complain, judge, and knock people down, then you my friend will become that person. If you want to lose weight, quit hanging out with people who don't value their health. Detoxing negative people that don't support you is hard; trust me I have had to do it. But the payoff is 100% worth it. Spend time with positive people, read self-development books, celebrate your wins, and listen to positive and empowering podcasts.

What is your best advice for women who want to lose weight, have more energy, and boost their confidence?

Karissa Adkins: Figure out your why, know why you want to change. Work with a professional if you need the help, whether it's a coach, therapist, trainer, or nutritionist — get help where you need it. Get an accountability partner who will push you beyond your comfort zone so that you can reach higher levels.

What makes you and your services stand out from other trainers and professionals?

Karissa Adkins: What makes me different from other coaches is that I walk the walk and talk the talk. I have been in my client's shoes and I know how hard it can be to BossUp and create a better life. I am real and authentic, and I call BS when I hear it, and my clients appreciate that. My programs don't just focus on one aspect of health such as nutrition or exercise. My programs focus on total mind body wellness and teaching women how to create healthy habits that will support them forever. Me and my team are made up of health coaches, healers, trainers, and nutritionist and I believe that this is what truly sets my programs apart. It's a high touch high accountability program that leaves no women behind.

As a motivational speaker, what are your favorite topics to discuss on podcasts and webinars and write about in blogs?

Karissa Adkins: I love motivating people to BossUp, Show Up and Thrive. My favorite subjects to talk about are health and wellness, resiliency, mindset, and habit change. Two of my favorite talks are called "From Blah to Badass, How to BossUp and Get healthy" and "From Hot mess to Boss Success"

What is the best way to reach out to you?

Karissa Adkins: You can find me online at my website 365DailyHustle.com. My IG handle is 365.Daily.Hustle and my Facebook group is called *The Healthy Hustle* which is for women looking to thrive and create a healthier life. My coaching program is called *Reclaim Your Best Life*, which is a 10-week transformational program that will help women overcome their weight loss battle, double their energy, self-doubt, and self-sabotaging spirals while they learn to master their mind, habits, confidence, and own their true badass self. If you're ready to awaken the sexy, powerful, unstoppable queen that I know is inside of you then the Reclaim your Best Life program is for you.

About Karissa Adkins

Karissa Adkins is a certified Life, Health, and Mastery Coach through Health Coach Institute, certified Personal Trainer through NAFTA, Global motivational speaker, Radio show host of BossUp Babe Radio, Founder and CEO of 365 Daily Hustle, and a Co-Author of "Women Who BossUp!"

Karissa is able to bring practical real-world experience to her coaching, mentoring, and speaking engagements. She believes that personal and professional development go hand in hand when it comes to living a happy, healthy, and successful life. She also understands the daily struggles that many women navigate as they attempt to live a more balanced life. Karissa truly enjoys speaking and teaching women how to "Boss Up" and rise above their current situation. Her signature talks are guaranteed to leave the audience feeling empowered, motivated, and inspired to level up in a way like never before.

WEBSITE
365DailyHustle.com

EMAIL
Karissa@365DailyHustle.com

FACEBOOK GROUP
Facebook.com/groups/365healthyhustle/

INSTAGRAM
365.daily.hustle

OTHER
https://linktr.ee/365dailyhustle

REAL ESTATE PROFITABILITY®
SERIOUS MONEY. EVERY DEAL.

Creating wealth through Real Estate is the best way to create lasting legacy wealth! After more than 30 years of real estate experience, Leslie Purdy, a seasoned real estate investor who still buys, holds, flips, and rehabs properties answers questions in this interview about how she is a successful real estate investor.

Leslie Purdy is a third-generation real estate investor who started learning about construction at two years old when she was a tool fetcher for her father as he remodeled their family home.

At age 10, Leslie helped their parents repair and renovate their rental houses. At 14, she helped rehab commercial property. By age 22, she had become a land-lord while attending Florida State University.

Since 1995, Leslie and her husband, Sean, slow-flipped the houses they lived in and remodeled their rentals. In 2002, Leslie earned her real estate license and sold more than 20-plus houses each year for clients, adding to her vast knowledge of real estate. In 2013, she started to rehab houses full time. By 2020, Leslie and Sean had increased their net worth exponentially: retaining more than half of their flips as rental properties. Leslie now shares her expertise with many students through mentoring while still improving properties, managing rentals, and helping clients achieve their dreams.

Conversation with Leslie Purdy

What inspired you to become a real estate mentor?

Leslie Purdy: Over the years, I helped my clients and investors buy and sell investment properties. After purchasing the properties, they came to me for advice about how to handle things. My advice worked! My parents were real estate investors, so I decided to take my parents' lead. My mother has been my greatest influence. When I was a teenager, she bought ten rentals. My dad had me entering checks into a Mac, and I learned about bookkeeping when I was 14 years old.

Now, I love real estate because it creates multiple streams of income. I had an epiphany when I was 43. I realized that retirement was never going to happen until I made some changes about how I thought about money and how I use that money as a tool to create investments that I could control.

The big bonus for me is that I like teaching others how to save time and money while running an efficient business. I realized that I could help others save time and money by sharing my trial-and-error stories. Trial and error is a big part of real estate. The beauty of having a real estate mentor is that if somebody is thinking about doing real estate investment, or real estate flipping, they don't need to go through all the ups and downs because I have already done it.

How should someone evaluate a real estate mentor?

Leslie Purdy: The most important thing investors should consider when evaluating a real estate investor mentor is their track record. Ask a lot of questions. Can your prospective mentor prove that they own properties and that they have had hands-on experience working the deal? You may want to compare the mentor's investments versus where you are planning to put your investment. You have to be prepared to work on your real estate projects daily, so make sure that your mentor is available daily if you have any questions or have any emergencies.

As a mentor, what advice do you have for a novice investor?

Leslie Purdy: My advice for a novice investor is to do something. You have to get prepared and do your homework. Start small by flipping a mobile home or lower-value property. Test yourself to see how you react to risk and the flipping process.

Start small, so you can learn how to run your numbers and practice all the steps involved like home inspections, surveys, working with contractors, and so forth. Practice with different scenarios and run your numbers to see what happens. For example, what happens if the house doesn't sell quickly? What happens if

I rent it? Will I have enough money to cover all the expenses? Will I have enough to pay back the lender? Can I cover all my costs? You can waylay many fears just by running your numbers!

What is Real Estate Profitability?

Leslie Purdy: I love helping people save time and money by creating efficient systems. I teach my students to make good money on every deal. Investing in anything is a numbers game. As a mentor, I provide tools to crunch those numbers accurately. I give people the tools to determine whether a deal will be as lucrative as they hope. Many people have a hard time estimating the unknown. If you don't have a lot of experience with it, it can be challenging. This is where the experience of dealing with so many properties comes in handy. I can help with estimating and provide guidance in helping them find the right people to get good estimates. Every house is different, and there will be challenges. My comprehensive system helps people figure out these challenges, usually before they even come up.

I work with anybody who wants to flip a house anywhere. I also can teach them about landlording. Housing is generally the same around the world. It's not rocket science, but it is challenging. Things need to be done in a certain way to create that profit every month on every deal.

As a real estate mentor, do you have any examples of how you have helped some of your clients with their projects?

Leslie Purdy: As a real estate mentor, I coach people through their deals. Since every house is different, a real estate investor lays out the scenario, and I help them find a suitable solution that will make the most money. It is essential to diversify your investments. Don't put all your eggs in one basket. Buy houses in different neighborhoods. I also recommend that you work with various contractors. Loyalty is great, but at the same time, you may be pigeon-holing yourself with one contractor when another one would do the job more efficiently for less money.

Discuss your first real estate investment experience?

Leslie Purdy: My first investing experience as an adult was buying a house in Tallahassee, while attending Florida State University. We bought that house for about $30,000. It was 1996, and I had a great state job with lots of benefits. Luckily, my mom helped and guided me through the purchase of that house. My mom was my first mentor.

It was an FHA loan at 6% interest with Regions Bank. The principal and interest on that mortgage were around $350 a month. We lived in that house for about a year and then moved back to my hometown five hours away. It was tough to manage the rental from so far away, but we had friends who could help us keep an eye on the place and deal with the tenants short term. Luckily, the very first tenant we moved in ended up buying the house seven years later, for double what we had paid. Since we were paying the entire rent payment of $450 toward the mortgage each month, the loan was almost paid off. In this case, the tenant paid for the house three times. With this first investment, we were almost able to pay off the house, and in seven years, we sold it for double our initial investment. That was an amazing lesson for me: it was worth it to retain the property as a landlord for seven years and then sell it for a substantial profit.

What is the most important lesson you learned from your first rental investment that still affects your business today?

Leslie Purdy: The big lesson is that you have to have a reliable manager who lives near the property. You have to have someone who is tried and true. You need to trust your property manager to follow through and check on the property regularly.

Another vital tip is to pay off your loans as quickly as possible. You can save exponentially by not paying interest. Another critical factor is always qualifying your tenants well and keeping in communication with them every few months. We like to inspect each of our houses every six months.

I see my tenants twice a year in person at the property. Using this schedule helps us. This lets you know if there are any problems with the house, or if the tenants are not maintaining the property as per the lease agreement.

Over the years, you have flipped more than 60 houses; what are some of the mistakes or failures that you've experienced over this time?

Leslie Purdy: The worst flip we ever did was while we were under contract for a property, and a few days before closing, the title company told us the payoff on the home was $15,000 higher than what the seller initially told us. If we wanted that house, we would have to pay that extra $15,000. In this case, the house only needed some basic cosmetics like painting; we ended up buying it and making about $10,000 for two weeks of work.

Typically, our profit would have been about $30,000 for a month's worth of work. While we didn't make a big profit, we did make something. At least we didn't lose money!

What is the biggest lesson you have learned that you can attribute to your ongoing daily success?

Leslie Purdy: The biggest lesson we have is to be prepared to walk away from a deal. When the numbers change unexpectedly, you have to be ready to walk away. Always be sure you are working with a good title company. It is essential to have a proactive title company. If the title company had run that title search earlier and not in the last week before closing, we would have had more time to negotiate. You have to either negotiate or walk away. At the time, I didn't walk away because I had a crew that I needed to keep busy with work. It is important to keep a full-time crew working and busy. You don't want to lose your good crew by running out of work.

If you could go back in time, what advice would you give yourself?

Leslie Purdy: The big lesson I learned from the real estate crash in 2010 was to downsize in an upmarket and upsize in a down market. That means to sell your big house when the markets are high and move to a smaller house when the market is low. The bigger and more expensive properties are easily attainable in a down market because fewer people want to do the work or can afford to do the work. If you have finances built up, or at least the option to borrow at that point, it makes a lot of sense to buy as many houses as you can in the down market.

What is the most important factor when someone is evaluating real estate investments?

Leslie Purdy: Numbers never lie. Always run your numbers and evaluate the property. Do this by running comparables of similar properties in the neighborhood.

Is there any difference in evaluating properties during up and down economies?

Leslie Purdy: run Always run the numbers. Every deal has positives and negatives. When you run the numbers, you can figure out if the positives are enough for you to take that risk, especially when you consider what may happen in the next six months in the real estate market.

What professionals should you have to help you with your real estate investments besides a good real estate mentor?

Leslie Purdy: Everyone should have a team of professionals to help them navigate the ins and outs of real estate investing. You need a good foundational office team that includes an accountant, attorney, title company, surveyor, home inspector, and assistant.

Your home inspector is very important. They can make or break you. If they miss wood rot, pests, or other issues in a house, it can cost you big money. Here is a tip: have the property inspected before you make the offer. A good local real estate attorney is essential. Check around and ask others in your area for recommendations and always check their online reviews. You want to have a reliable team working with you. Ask for recommendations around your local area and look for five-star reviews online. Always get references.

What profit margin should people be aiming for when they invest in real estate?

Leslie Purdy: Typically, 20% profit right off the top. I will not pay the retail price for a property. I always look for mistakes in the listing, such as the wrong square footage. For example, maybe the house is larger than what the listing says. What excites me is when I find unused spaces or poorly designed floor plans that could be adjusted to make a better flow in the house. For instance, sometimes there is a carport or garage. Many people don't use their carport or garage space in Florida, so it could be turned into a separate apartment if there is a water source. With the market growing and a housing shortage, there is a huge opportunity to create multi-family housing. This could be useful for your family members. Many families have multi-generations living in their homes. Sometimes adult children move in, or parents move in with their children to help out with rent and other bills.

What is the first thing you do to improve a living space?

Leslie Purdy: I would try and create the most usable space for the least amount of money, earning us the most significant profit. For instance, on one of our existing properties, we had to move the laundry room to the kitchen because the house was built with the laundry off of the bedroom. You had to go outside through the carport to get to the laundry room. That's no longer fashionable like it was in the 1960s, so we moved the laundry area into the kitchen because it was the best use of the space. We ended up turning the carport into an apartment by using the water source from the old laundry room for the bathroom, and it helped create a mother-in-law space and an increase in rent of $600 a month.

With real estate profitability and flipping houses, what would you say are the big advantages and benefits you see in becoming a real estate investor house flipper?

Leslie Purdy: There are a lot of positives about rehabbing houses. My favorite is that I get to be creative. I can design and create a gorgeous house that everyone wants to buy from a crappy worn out property that all the neighbors hated. It creates buzz around the neighborhood. The neighbors are happy when the property gets fixed up. It creates goodwill. Selling a property to make

$30,000 to $50,000 in profit is also an excellent way to improve your life. It's addicting.

What are the biggest myths surrounding real estate, investing in house flipping?

Leslie Purdy: I found that a lot of my success has come from my ability to handle multiple tasks throughout the day. You don't have to be a man to run a construction crew; you have to be able to communicate and check on them. If you use other people's money (OPM), you have nothing to lose, supposedly. However, when you use other people's money, you will have to invest something yourself, either your time or your money. Sometimes, up to 20% of the deal is the requirement, or you're paying exorbitant interest rates. There is always some risk.

Many gurus say to use other people's money and claim you're not risking anything, but you are, you're risking the deal, and your time. Any investment of time, energy, or money you have in the property could disappear if you don't handle it right. Another misconception is related to how long it takes to flip a house. If it's a fast deal, and you've got everybody coordinated adequately, it could take two months. Or three months from the time you close on the purchase to the time you close on the sale. I have had properties take up to a year for that to happen. Everything depends on the coordination of the crew, subcontractors, permits, etc. It depends on how much rehab you need to do. You have to realize you won't make $50,000 on every deal. Think about repeating the process every three months and keep a tight rein so you can keep everything running smoothly. You can make a lot more money flipping houses than working a nine to five job, but it takes a lot of effort to make it work.

What are some fears and misconceptions that investors have related to real estate?

Leslie Purdy: The one that comes to mind right now is that many would-be investors might getting into the market when it's high in case it drops.

Some investor fears revolve around the concept of personal risk. In anything, there is the risk of losing money with every deal, so you have that personal risk. To mitigate risk, it is vital to know your numbers. A real estate mentor can help you become successful by providing you with someone to discuss your options to make the right decisions about properties in which to invest.

How can people reach you?

Leslie Purdy: Talk/text me at 321-209-INFO (4636). Connect with me: www.MeetLeslie.com.

Contact Leslie Purdy

WEBSITE
LesliePurdy.com and RealEstateProfitability.com

FACEBOOK
Facebook.com/REProfitability

TALK/TEXT:
321-209-4636

TRUE FIT MARKETING – FOUNDATIONAL MARKETING METHODOLOGY

Arlea Hoffman is the owner of True Fit Marketing®, a full-service marketing advocacy firm powered by technology and grounded with foundational marketing based out of Pittsburgh, PA, supporting clientele nationwide. "Simple. Authentic. Unique. Marketing that Fits. Naturally. Our goal is to help you feel more confident and support your team in your marketing efforts!"

True Fit Marketing promises to support you, your business, and your team, while helping you feel more confident in your marketing efforts. Their objective is to help you tell your story authentically and uniquely while also teaching you to use a variety of media to give your business a foundation to stand on. True Fit Marketing partners with the best local and national teams to give you trusted quality without sacrificing your budget. With fully transparent reporting and consistent evaluation meetings, they want to be held accountable for helping your business succeed.

True Fit Marketing is excited to learn all about your marketing and business goals, business history, motivations, and the reason why you love your business and what you do every day. Then, they will work with you to develop a marketing strategy that best fits your business goals and personal style. Telling your story to the right people at the right time can be a very delicate task, but when you're ready, we'll be here to help guide you on your marketing journey!

Conversation with Arlea Hoffman

Tell us a little bit about True Fit Marketing and how you're helping your clients.

Arlea Hoffman: True Fit Marketing is, first and foremost, your marketing advocate. We are a full-service marketing agency, and we want to help educate you on your options, what those options can do for your business, and what reasonable timeframes to test return on investment are. All of those marketing pieces should also work together cohesively to give you the biggest advantage, so even implementing them to their full potential can be difficult. When it comes to your marketing and advertising, you can take advantage of so many different possibilities. You may also have other advertising opportunities presented to you as a small business owner or marketing representative. It's hard to know who to trust and what decisions to make. Our goal is to guide you.

We live in a world where we search Google for the answers we need when we need them. But having those answers show up when searches are happening can be an intricate and cohesive storytelling process, starting with the foundation marketing pieces of your business.

It is important to first evaluate and then be ready to showcase your brand, logo, website, and social media branding. Once this foundation is built, then you will start trying to drive qualified audiences with targeted advertising options.

While mastering those two areas, you also need to retain your current and new audience and keep them engaged with your brand. Programs like reputation management are important not only to know your on-line reputation, but also engage with those who leave reviews and create a process to continue gathering reviews on a regular basis. There are many pieces in each step of the process, but the final step is continuing to evaluate and adjust for success.

Many businesses get caught up in the "chasing the shiny new technology" mentality that if you are not doing it, you are behind and going to fail. In reality, it is creating good marketing foundations and processes that will lead you to success!

What are some of the benefits and advantages of providing transparency and reporting on marketing results for business owners? What do you do, how do you do it, and why?

Arlea Hoffman: Education is at the forefront of everything that we do. One of the first steps we take after your first month of marketing is reviewing in-depth reporting to ensure our businesses have a solid understanding of what the numbers mean. We try to make it very easy for business owners and marketing representatives to understand since there are so many analytics and reporting capabilities available. It's more important for the business owner to really understand their goals, how their marketing programs work together, and what that looks like as a return on investment.

Transparent reporting and no contracts on programs allow us to test different types of advertising and budgets for our clients to determine what formula works for them. No two businesses are alike. If something doesn't go well, that's actually not a bad thing because we now know that advertising avenue does not work towards our end goal, so we will adjust the budget. We need to take a look at the in-depth, transparent reporting to say, "Hey, this actually didn't work this month. We're going to move this budget over to this other program and try it out..." Marketing is a huge testing opportunity to see what formula works best, what doesn't, and continue adjusting towards success.

If an individual is not a savvy marketer or just starting out as a business owner, they don't know to take one piece and test it. Is it your mission to teach business owners?

Arlea Hoffman: Yes. Training and educating businesses is just as important to us as marketing. Working with clients, we provide many services ourselves, but our passion is to educate businesses and marketing specialists so they don't get taken advantage of by others trying to speak over their heads. We provide education both through the clients we work with directly and by partnering with local Chambers of Commerce, other credible marketing agencies, and even Google and Facebook representatives to help provide the best education and resources to our clients and the general business community.

What questions should small business owners ask and what are the costs associated with hiring a full-service marketing company?

Arlea Hoffman: Business owners often forget that it's a two-way relationship. So, not only should the partnership be good for the business itself, but it should also be good for the agency. An agency is much more likely to work hard for you if they enjoy the relationship. We tell businesses that is very important to find an agency that has the same vision and tone so that you enjoy your meetings and have fun together.

One of the best compliments we've ever received was from a client who said that every time we meet, they laugh the whole time and have such a good time. Our goal is to take the stress out of marketing and have fun telling stories that help promote our clients.

So, the relationship is one of the most important aspects of building an agency partnership. Many business owners also don't realize that you don't have to be locked into a contract. We do not have contracts because our goal every month is to relieve your stress. We find that in two to three months, we will know if the relationship is a good fit for both parties.

We are really transparent, so if we part ways, we can point you in the right direction. We do not have that happen very often because we evaluate the relationship from the beginning, but it's important to know that the business owner can find their own way and make those educated decisions if it does happen. Not holding our clients to contracts creates accountability for both sides. Our goal is to prove to you the success of your marketing campaigns.

If we're not willing and able to do that for you, then we are not the agency of choice for you. Ensure that you are comfortable and have decision-making options available to you.

The cost of working with an agency depends on the number of services that you have them take over. For example, we manage only the website and social media for some of our clients and manage tens of thousands of dollars in advertising budget for others. There are different costs based on the level of your marketing needs, your advertising budget, and the services required.

It's essential to know that the agency you're working with has your best intentions in mind. Many times, businesses can "feel" that almost immediately, but you will know within the first month if an agency is a good fit for you.

What are some of the common mistakes that you see small business owners make as they're growing their business?

Arlea Hoffman: There are two that come to mind immediately. First, they try to handle too much themselves and different pieces start to falter. So, our goal is to come in and eliminate the marketing stress so that the business or trade can do what they're best at. Also, many people try to work in several positions, such as CEO, the CFO, the IT person, the PR person, the marketing person. As the business grows, the goal should be to start delegating tasks to different trusted experts. If there is more to be done than you have time to do in your day, you need to be doing what you're good at, which is your business.

Second, a marketing relationship needs input from the business. Some of our businesses have marketing managers, and we support them. Some do not have any marketing help on staff, and we're the support team for that direct owner. For of our franchise clients, we are the support team helping to create localized marketing content for the business owner and we work closely with the corporate marketing team to ensure everything is on brand.

The first thing that we tell clients is you do need to be involved. You can't just give this to someone and have magic happen. There will be consistent meetings to help understand: How is your business growing? What conversations are you having with your customers? And what questions are you getting that we can help answer them more conveniently, especially with digital marketing resources? It is a balance of being involved and providing input, but also knowing it is being taken care of professionally and we will come to you with ideas and questions! Together, we will work to build the right marketing foundation for your business!

If you're going to delegate and take that step and take it off your plate and hand it over, then you absolutely must have that trust. Do you run into that issue a lot with clients?

Arlea Hoffman: Not often because we discuss whether we are the right fit for your goals. If you're going to be so involved that you're doing all the work, you shouldn't waste your money or resources on having us do it as well.

We also come across people who are ready to take that next step and don't want to be involved at all. Again, it's a balance. We still want to talk to you and have a conversation like the following at a minimum every month or two: "This is how your campaigns are going. Are you still hearing the conversations we've discussed before, or are there new conversations you're hearing?" It's so important to have a very balanced relationship. We're here to support, educate, and help you make right decisions because, ultimately, we want your business to grow.

What inspired you start a full-service marketing firm?

Arlea Hoffman: When I graduated from grad school, I was incredibly lucky enough to get a job as the director of marketing and communications for a sports and recreation facility. I worked closely with the advertising companies and marketing consultants. I was being locked into contracts and pushed towards programs that I now realize were the marketing consultant's sales goals and not those of our facilities. Did those programs help us? It was hard to tell, but ultimately those professionals were not being my advocate. They were trying to make their own sales goals. Some of the contracts at the time were for 3–5 years.

I heard story after story of other marketing managers and small business owners who were stuck in contracts and people talking over their heads, especially those offering new technologies that the general public didn't understand yet. So, after years of being a marketing director, I decided these people needed an advocate, and I truly didn't want others to be taken advantage of anymore. I continued to train myself (because I love marketing and advertising) and teach businesses how to make all of their marketing assets work well together. I also want them to know what questions to ask when consultants or advertising agencies approach them to spend their marketing budget.

We are passionate about education. For example, many people don't understand what they get when they are buying an advertising option. There might be some opportunities to negotiate variables like contact lengths, positions, and even deadlines if you need more time.

I am very blessed. True Fit Marketing is the sixth agency that I've helped launched across the country. I currently travel and train marketing agencies and small businesses in different parts of the country. We've worked really hard not only to help local businesses, but also to help agencies work with those businesses and create marketing advocacy firms in other parts of the country. We teach them how to work with businesses to build grass roots and local community/hyper local marketing programs that help businesses be successful for the long term. We teach them to ask questions like: Should you be a part of the local chamber? What makes your business a little bit different? Should you be sponsoring the local baseball team? We help research the opportunities for business community support that we can help build for you as well, right there, where you live.

When you started creating full-service marketing firms as an entrepreneur, what was the reaction from your friends and family? Did you have a job before?

Arlea Hoffman: I'm proud to say, which seems ridiculous, that my very first agency failed... and it needed to fail. I had to learn what I should know to be successful. I realized I had to find a full-time position again for the income and had an amazing opportunity to work full time for a media company that wanted me to develop an agency and a new digital marketing department.

My friends and family were so incredibly supportive, especially while building True Fit Marketing, and believe I have an entrepreneurial spirit. They think that there's a fire inside of me, and that I need to continue to be a passionate explorer, adventurer and educator, and keep learning and growing.

I've learned so much in this last decade about partnerships, support, and that it takes a grassroots and foundational marketing approach for businesses to be successful.

Many people say, "Oh, I wish I knew everything." I say, "That's hundreds of thousands of dollars and hours of education and hard knocks and figuring it out as you go!" What do you think?

Arlea Hoffman: The world of marketing is ever-changing. Every single day is similar, but different than the day before. We take it in stride and embrace that we know and accept that it's going to change, and we will adjust with it and continue to test and make sure that we're getting the best results.

What is a lesson you learned early on that still impacts how you do business today?

Arlea Hoffman: Honestly, the biggest lesson I learned is that nothing is set in stone. Whether it's how you think things will go, all the way up to technology and automations, everything constantly changes. For businesses, you have to accept that changes are normal and good for you and be ready to learn and adjust to the next best thing. It's always coming and always better, so you just have to find that light!

Just to remain flexible and remain somewhat stress-free, right?

Arlea Hoffman: Don't stress. That's what I tell my staff and our clients. If a client gets a bad review, no worries! We'll figure out what happened and how to make it right. Then you can create processes to help catch issues, which will ultimately help make everything better!

What are the most important questions small business owners should ask themselves as they consider hiring a full-service marketing firm or, if they should continue doing it themselves?

Arlea Hoffman: Question #1: Are they ready to hear "No?" That is not meant to sound harsh, but an expectation that the marketing needs might not be what they envisioned. Owners and even marketing reps have a very emotional investment in their business and their marketing, but how they consume marketing might be different from how their target audience consumes marketing. It's important to be ready to come in with an open mind to hear different ways to think about your marketing. Once we establish what the target market is, we can decide which messages to use and start testing different opportunities. Often, what that looks like is not what the business owner or marketing person expected.

Question #2-4: Are you ready to trust this agency with your business's reputation? Are you ready to have a relationship with this agency? Are you ready to take time to invest in them, learning about your business and really digging down to what works best for you?

Be patient and ready to have a relationship with a support team. If you have a good feeling about them, try it for a little while. Although you're emotionally invested in your business, it might not be what you expect when it comes to your marketing.

If somebody wants to find out more about Arlea Hoffman and True Fit Marketing and how you can help them, where should they go

Arlea Hoffman: You can find us on all of our social media handles: @TrueFitMarketing and you can also go to our website at https://TrueFitMarketing.com. If you want to learn more about our team, visit our "About Our Team" page. It takes a village to create a support team! We're happy to chat with anyone who needs some support or even a push in the right direction. We'll be here when you need us.

About Arlea Hoffman

Arlea Hoffman is the founder and owner of True Fit Marketing. She has launched six marketing agencies all across the country. Arlea's favorite "job" is being a mom to her two little bears, and she likes to say that her family keeps her centered and down to earth. Arlea's professional passion is business and marketing. Because she has sat on both sides of the desk (marketing director and marketing consultant), Arlea enjoys educating and helping businesses navigate the constantly changing world of advertising, reputation, and online marketing.

Prior to the lift-off of True Fit Marketing, Arlea was honored to develop, launch, and be the Digital Strategy Director of a nationally award-winning digital agency. She has worked in a marketing capacity, locally and nationally, for over ten years. This includes leading a team of local digital strategists and managing national business partners from across the country who are experts in their respective fields.

Arlea's passion for marketing education is derived from conversations with clients who have been overwhelmed with the vast amount of marketing and advertising options and are unsure where they should start and who to trust. She loves to educate business owners and marketers by partnering with local chambers of commerce, networking groups, and community organizations so when local businesses are approached by marketing companies, they understand what questions to ask, and they feel prepared and confident in their marketing decisions.

Her passion for digital marketing started in the early 2000s when she became fascinated with the possibilities created by coding, including reporting capabilities unmatched by any other existing marketing platform. With the evolution of digital marketing, she continues to provide innovative opportunities to help her clients grow.

At heart, Arlea is a very geeky country girl, lover of laughing, and enjoys traveling nationally to speak on a variety of marketing and agency topics. She and her family love nature, hiking, playing sports, animals and currently live in the country outside of Pittsburgh.

Arlea is truly thankful for the opportunity to own a marketing firm that helps deliver inspiration and education to businesses in a field that can be confusing to navigate.

WEBSITE

TrueFitMarketing.com

ADDRESS

Pittsburgh, PA

PHONE

(412) 561-3302

EMAIL

team@truefitmarketing.com

FACEBOOK

Facebook.com/TrueFitMarketing

DIAMOND FACTOR EXPERIENCE

Barbara Beckley is a successful professional speaker, best-selling author, and social media and purpose strategist with more than seven years of experience. She can help you find the diamond inside of you and help make you shine. She is skilled in assisting people in creating an online presence to be seen professionally on social media platforms. Barbara is the founder and CEO of the Diamond Factor, LLC. She helps people understand their purpose, passion and drive and move forward despite the trials and challenges in their lives.

Conversation with Barbara Beckley

How does having purpose, passion, and drive help people to move forward in their lives?

Barbara Beckley: We all need a foundation in our lives. I have found in what I call PPD: your purpose, passion, and drive. You genuinely need to understand what's in your heart and your motivations and know that deep down that you are here for a reason. Every person is here for a purpose. You are on this Earth because you are a tool concerning the gifts and talents within you. When you understand PPD, you are more motivated because you are standing on a solid foundation and can move forward no matter what is happening around you.

In 2020, the world certainly was shaken up, and we all have our stories. Can you help us understand how our stories guide us to become who we are supposed to become?

Barbara Beckley: We all have our storms. We all go through particular challenges in our lives. It's a choice. You can let things overtake you and not move forward, or you can move forward and dismiss the storm around you that causes you to stop. You can ask yourself questions like, "What am I going to do?" Instead of looking at yourself as a victim of circumstances, you can use your challenges and obstacles as steppingstones and learning techniques in your life. It moves you to believe whatever is happening will strengthen you. Some people go around it; some people go over it, and others go through the storm. When they do, they say, "Wow, I did it! I'm still here." Once you go through that storm called life, you give other people hope when they witness you dealing with it. That is why I love telling my stories. I do not have a problem being vulnerable because it creates a connection for someone and gives them hope for their own challenges. They could say, "If Barbara went through it, I could get through it, too." Stories help you understand life processes. When you go through those storms, those hurricanes. You can look at your life and say, "It's not just for me anymore. It's for others, too, so they know they can get through it."

How do you find your talents and gifts?

Barbara Beckley: It's a process. When I mentor others, I ask them, "What do you truly love? When you wake up in the morning, what do you think about?" For example, a person might state, "I like to teach children. I want to see them grow." I like to see the "aha" moments in their face when they're learning different things.

Then at night, when you go to bed, what do you think about it? Write these things down and ask yourself what excites and motivates you? What you would do that you could do all day long, day after day, and want to do it still over and over again. I always suggest that people start a journal and write down everything — all the little things. Some people like to organize. Others want to clean. Become aware of what your gifts and talents are. Take a look at yourself, and you will see that gift or talent shining in front of you. It's like that little light at the end of the tunnel directing you to your true purpose and passion.

How did you develop the Diamond Factor? How is it relevant to others?

Barbara Beckley: The Diamond Factor LLC does have a story behind it. It's not about just being big and shiny — there's a deeper story. Between ages six and eight, I was heavily bullied in school. The children would say I was ugly and stupid. They would say they didn't understand why I was going to school because I wouldn't amount to anything. Every day, these children would tell me I was worthless. I would go home crying. My dad was home in the afternoon because he worked in the early mornings. He would give me the biggest bear hug and ask, *"What's wrong?"* I told him about the bullies at school and how they told me I was ugly and stupid.

My dad said, "I want you to remember one thing. I'm going to remind you every single day that you are just a diamond in the rough. You are getting molded. Some things are going to happen that will be hurtful at times. Still, you're going to become a beautiful diamond that is going to shine within not just for yourself, but everybody else around you is going to see that diamond in you."

When I was young, I knew a diamond was pretty, but I didn't understand what he meant until he passed away. My father always put positive words in me to keep me moving forward. I studied hard. When I was 17, my father was murdered. He was my diamond. I was distraught, and they admitted me to the hospital on suicide watch.

A nurse came into the room. She looked at me as she did my vitals.

She said, "I don't know what you're thinking about right now, Barbara; I know somebody in your life passed away. Something is telling me that they would not want you to take your life away. Something in me is saying that you are a diamond, like a diamond in the rough."

When she said that, everything in me telling me that I should end it, changed. Everything just clicked. Her words were the sound of my dad telling me, *"You're a diamond in a rough, and you're going to be a great big shining diamond. When you get older, and people are going to see that from you. You're going to resonate with people. You're going to help people!"* At that moment in time, I told myself that I have to make sure that others know that they have a diamond in them. That's why I called my brand and my business Diamond Factor LLC.

You have an acronym called BUILD. What positive action steps are the most powerful to help someone get through their life storms and hurricanes?

Barbara Beckley: I'm always talking about building your strength, the steppingstones of strength and moving forward. I thought about build; we have to build our lives. So, B-U-I-L-D became my acronym of steppingstones or action steps. First, you have to believe in yourself and be bold. You must believe that you are beautiful, intelligent, wonderful — it starts from within you. Each person is unique, so I use the U from the word "Unique."

Every person has gifts, talents and each individual is unique. When you are amazing and authentic, you will attract people to you because of who you are.

The letter I is for invest. Invest in yourself. L is for active listening and learning. And D is for direction and development. Make sure you develop an action plan, a guide for your life for what you're trying to do. It is vital that you build your own life and not try to run someone else's race.

How do you help people focus on their social media presence?

Barbara Beckley: First, I coach them to dig deep to find their purpose, passion, and drive. I resonate because of life experiences. I also help my clients focus on messaging and social media strategies.

What is the most important thing for people to think about when developing that consistent message for their branding and marketing?

Barbara Beckley: People must understand their passion, purpose, and drive to have social media strategy that attracts their ideal clients. It's important to ask questions such as:

What is the happiest thing in your life?
What makes you happy?
What makes you proud?

I listen to people and go from there to help them develop their plans for branding and messaging.

What obstacles do you see that stop people from seeing or accepting their purpose?

Barbara Beckley: The two things that I've seen a lot are that people doubt themselves and fear. I can share some tools to help people overcome those feelings. For example, you can change your mindset. If you doubt yourself, you can use affirmations regularly and you will be amazed at how much you will change your words to positive. Fear is another problem for many people. They get stuck. Fear and self-doubt can stop you from moving onto your true purpose.

What other tools would you say would be necessary for finding a person's purpose and that drive?

Barbara Beckley: Start the process by asking yourself questions. What are your interests? What are your beliefs? What are your values?

Secondly, find affirmations that resonate with you and your goals. Once you have answered your questions, you can create a personal mission statement. Just like a business has a mission statement, each person can have a mission statement that helps them move forward and live their big why!

What would you like people to understand about being a diamond?

Barbara Beckley: Make sure that you are being human. You must be who you are. It's so important because there is a person out there looking for you to help them make an impact in their lives.

I want to end it with this story. I posted something three months ago on social media. I talked a little bit about what I went through when my father passed, and was thinking about suicide, how I struggled with his death, and the miracle nurse who came in and echoed his words to me. I always want to connect to someone who needs to hear this, and I sent out my prayers that someone will listen to this, and it will help them.

Five days later, someone shared my post on Facebook. You never know who will share it or where it will go. I received a message from a young lady who was 17 or 18 years old. She was about the same age I was when my father passed. She told me that she was thinking about ending her life with a knife when she heard my post. She said, "I told myself, I don't want to do this. I think that this is a mistake. I want to live."

It put tears in my heart as she told me this. We must all share our stories. This tells you how important one person can be to someone else. Each of us can make an impact. So, I want everybody to know that you need to understand your PPD because it important for you to know and you can also save lives and help others.

Where can people get more information, if they would like to contact you to work with you, or get more basic information about the Diamond Factor?

Barbara Beckley: Contact me via email at diamondfactorexperience@gmail.com

Tell us more about your TV show and how someone can become a guest on it.

Barbara Beckley: The TV show is called "The Diamond Factor Experience with Barbara Beckley," and is featured on e360TV. You can contact me by email at diamondfactorexperience@gmail.com.

The Diamond Factor Experience Show showcases individuals with a business or unique passion for increasing their visibility. The three main points for the show is bringing awareness, motivating and educating the listener, and bringing motivation into a person's life.

About Barbara Beckley

Barbara Beckley is a successful professional speaker, best-selling author, and social media and purpose strategist with over seven years of experience. She can help you find the diamond inside of you and making you shine. She is skilled in assisting people in creating an online presence to be seen professionally on all social media platforms.

Barbara is the founder and CEO of the Diamond Factor LLC. She helps people understand their purpose, passion, and drive and move forward despite the trials and challenges in their lives. Barbara understands how it feels to be uncertain, confused, depressed, and sad. She lost her father, the rock of her world, to a murder when she was 17 years old. She is a conqueror of sexual abuse and a cancer conqueror for over nine years. Barbara can identify with people's struggles since she has been through trials of her own and survived. She can understand the eternal pain, insecurities, and how people search for their purpose because she has walked that journey.

Barbara understands what the world expects of people and how they are supposed to be strong and able to take on any challenge while they feel like crumbling inside. There is a way to turn this pain into strength, and Barbara knows how because she has done it herself. Through her trials, a spark was ignited, and her passion became to help others find that diamond that exists inside of them and turn their struggles and trial into power and strength. Barbara was able to take all those situations and turn them into the service-orientated person she is today. These struggles do not define who she is and make her story more compelling and her passion stronger to help others find their way.

EMAIL
diamondfactorexperience@gmail.com

FACEBOOK
Facebook.com/groups/DiamondFactorBB

WEBSITE
BarbaraBeckley.com

KATIE BRUNO, CFP®, CDFA, MIMFA

FINANCIAL PEACE OF MIND

Katie Bruno, a CERTIFIED FINANCIAL PLANNER Professional™ and Certified Divorce Financial Analyst, with Morey & Quinn Wealth Partners, is passionate about improving the financial lives of women and empowering them to make smart, thoughtful financial decisions. What Katie brings to her financial planning practice is a gift for building relationships and genuine concern for where people are in their lives. She is experienced and interested in the capital markets while understanding that each client's situation is unique and there is no one investment strategy that is the same for every client.

While Katie serves a very diverse group of clients, she specializes in working with women facing immediate financial decisions as a result of life-changing events. Her disciplined process involves meeting clients where they are, figuring out where they want to go, and creating a roadmap to meet their unique needs. She helps her clients through education, advocacy, and planning.

Many of Katie's clients come to her with financial questions to make decisions after losing a spouse, being forced to retire, or going through a divorce. Do they have enough income to support their family? Are they able to retire, or are they on track to retire? Is their future protected? What kind of investments and insurance do they have and/or may need?

Katie believes everyone deserves guidance from a team of professionals, regardless of the amount of money. The real value of a professional is helping you live a better life.

Katie holds a bachelor's degree in Business Management and a master's degree in Investment Management and Financial Analysis, both from Creighton University. In addition being a CFP® and CDFA, she holds a Series 7, 66 ,9, and 10 and Nebraska Life, Annuity, and Health Insurance licenses. She is a passionate and committed leader in the Omaha community, where you can find her in leadership roles with the Omaha Jaycees, 100 Women Who Care Omaha, Omaha Public Library Foundation, Financial Planning Association of Nebraska, and the Creighton University Recent Alumni Advisory Board.

When Katie isn't working with clients, she enjoys cheering on the Bluejays, reading, traveling, crafts, and spending time with friends and family.

Feel free to reach out to Katie if you or someone you know could benefit from having a conversation with a grounded and personable CERTIFIED FINANCIAL PLANNER™ Professional.

Conversation with Katie Bruno,
CFP®, CDFA, MIMFA

How did you become interested in becoming a financial planner?

KATIE BRUNO, CFP®, CDFA: I am a CERTIFIED FINANCIAL PLANNER™ Professional. I'm also a Certified Divorce Financial Analyst. A Certified Divorce Financial Analyst is someone who works with couples who are going through a divorce. There are many financial decisions that need to be made when couples separate. As someone who specializes in divorce, I can help with dividing the assets and making the divorce equitable in financial terms. Divorce and money bring up many emotions, so having a third party who isn't involved in the divorce emotionally there to walk you through and educate you using math is useful.

When I started in this business in 2013, I had no experience with money. My parents lived paycheck to paycheck and never saved much money. I didn't even understand the concept of an Individual Retirement Account (IRA), or a savings account. When I was in college, I wanted to get a summer job that would keep me in Omaha, so I applied for an internship with a financial advisor. My summer job project was to make his office paperless. I started teaching myself about all of the documents I was scanning, and I quickly became fascinated. From there, I became an assistant and grew to become a paraplanner, which is the person behind the scenes building the financial plans, explaining it all to the clients and working with the clients. I realized that I was doing a lot of the work of a financial advisor, and that realization was what I needed to make the next step in becoming an advisor. One of the best parts about this job is getting to see people enjoy the rewards of their money and wealth.

Who do you serve as a financial advisor?

KATIE BRUNO, CFP®, CDFA: I am passionate about helping women feel comfortable with making decisions around their money. I think there are a lot of misconceptions and fears. Once I started working in this business, I discovered that women need guidance and need someone to help educate them on their finances. Nobody is born knowing what a credit score is, why you shouldn't pay for things using a credit card, what a retirement account is, or how to grow and invest their money.

For me, it starts with education. Education is the foundation upon which we put together a plan and then follow it. My client base is very diverse. I particularly enjoy working with women going through life-changing events, whether that's a divorce, losing a spouse, or being forced to retire. Even more recently, the pandemic has caused many people to lose their jobs and not know what to do next. It is so important to educate people and help them create a plan. Financial planning leaves people with a renewed sense of hope. When you have a plan, you understand that while you can't control everything that has happened, you can take control of the path forward. That's the glimmer of hope that I get to help provide to my clients through this process.

Can you explain a bit more about some pitfalls people face as life events happen?

KATIE BRUNO, CFP®, CDFA: The first question many people have when a major life even happens is, "How am I going to pay my bills?" Generally speaking, that's the first question we need to answer. We have to review the income and cash flow coming in. Then, we need to ask, "How much are you spending?" One of the financial pitfalls we may talk about is possibly not having enough cash on hand due to divorce or widowhood.

We also need to look at our mindset. As time goes by and your mindset changes from lack to abundance, you can start making longer-term financial decisions, such as, "Am I on track to retire?" Many widows have no idea about paying bills because their spouse always took care that. So, we start with the things we need to do every day, and once we grasp that, we move on to learning and taking care of other financial tasks. It is important to discuss bill paying, retirement, insurance and risk planning, tax planning and estate planning. These are some of the heart-to-heart conversations a financial planner has with their clients.

What are the benefits of working with a financial advisor? Why is it important for these financial plans to be personalized?

KATIE BRUNO, CFP®, CDFA: When personalizing financial plans, I consider two things. First, your goals are not everyone else's goals, so that where the process begins. For example, one person might want to travel three times a year and spend $10,000 per trip, while another person might want to buy a vacation home, and another person might want to have a quiet retirement. Financial planning requires that we talk about individual goals. Once we know the client's goals, we can create an investment strategy designed to help meet those needs.

Another benefit of working with a financial advisor is developing discipline. An advisor can help someone follow a plan. When you have a financial advisor, you have a financial coach who wants you to be successful, holds you accountable to your goals, and helps you understand and deal with the emotional side to money. When someone looks at their 401(K), or retirement account and sees it going up and down, they tend to make emotional decisions. A financial advisor can help you eliminate some of those impulsive, emotional decisions based on the day-to-today "noise" in the financial industry.

Since there is an emotional side to money and investing, what are some of the most common fears people have about finances?

In the last eight years, I have discovered that people often don't use a financial advisor because they think it requires having a lot of money. That's simply not true. There's an advisor out there who wants to work with everyone. If you haven't found one yet, keep looking. Financial planning isn't designed only for the ultra-wealthy or the wealthy. Everyone needs to see a financial advisor so that they can build wealth. We are all on our own timelines.

Another fear that keeps people from using a financial advisor is the fear of failure or embarrassment about their financial situation. Money is a taboo topic, and fits into the same categories as sex, politics, religion. We are afraid to talk about it because we don't want to be embarrassed or feel judged about a poor decision we made or have to be compared to our peers.

The only way we can move forward from fear is by having more open and honest discussions about our money. For example, when you're out with your friends, ask how they might handle a particular situation or if they contribute to a 401k or other investments. We can have conversations about money without sharing too much personal information. We're going to move forward by having open conversations and educating each other.

The last fear that comes up often during planning meetings is that they don't have enough money saved. While this goes along with embarrassment and failure, it's also about feeling stupid. They don't want to look foolish or feel like they're asking questions they should know the answers to.

The truth is we don't learn financial literacy. It's not taught in most schools today. Often, we learn about money from our parents, which can be good or bad. Our parents teach us a lot of things subconsciously that we don't realize. It's important that we start teaching our kids about money to improve how people view money moving forward in their lives.

Is it ever too late to get a financial plan?

KATIE BRUNO, CFP®, CDFA: It is never too late. The best time to do something is now. Get started now — even if you are in your 50s, 60s, or 70s. The best decision is to take action. If you don't know the action to take, meet with a financial advisor to discuss what you can do. I have had consultations with clients in their

60s and 70s who want to retire but can't because they have a lot of debt. So, they may come to me for a retirement plan, and they end up leaving with a debt reduction plan, and that's okay. We are all on our own timeline, and it's important to make progress.

I also have clients who come to me thinking they are not in a situation to retire and they leave my office knowing they can financially retire the next day if they want to. There are different ways; it's never too late to meet with an advisor. Your timeline determines how we might approach something, given your resources and your circumstances.

What is the organization 100 Women Who Care Omaha?

KATIE BRUNO, CFP®, CDFA: The 100 Women Care Omaha is a growing, giving circle. Our goal for 100 women in our local community to each make a $100 donation to help charities that serve our local communities. When 100 women come together to give, that $100 donation turns into $10,000 and can make a sizable impact on local nonprofits.

Do you have any webinars or training about financial planning for women?

KATIE BRUNO, CFP®, CDFA: I have taught classes about the financial aspects of divorces for Divorce

Attorneys. I have also been interviewed on a local talk show focused on women's empowerment. I also offer monthly blogs and webinars on my social media platforms. I am always open to interviews and more opportunities to educate and advocate.

What would the process look like to start working with a financial planner or a financial advisor?

KATIE BRUNO, CFP®, CDFA: First, you must do your homework. You want to work with someone who has your best interest at heart. I live by the mantra that "People don't care what you know until they know that you care."

When you are selecting a financial advisor, interview them to find out about their processes. Ask how they get compensated and what types of investments they use. It's also important to know how frequently you can expect to hear from them.

Find someone whose values are aligned with yours and with whom you will feel comfortable with having open, honest, and vulnerable conversations about money. Interview at least a couple of different financial advisors so that you can feel confident with your choice.

My process starts with an introductory conversation. I don't follow a strict agenda during I have this first conversation because what I really want to get to know the person, who they are, and figure out their goals. I always cover the basics in our initial conversation which includes who I am and an overview on my business and how I am compensated. After that initial consultation or conversation, I'll put together a plan moving forward for a second or third meeting. We want to establish a timeline to get things accomplished. Remember, there's a difference between procrastination and making an educated, thoughtful decision. Take your time, do your research, and find someone that feels right.

What would you say is like the one big problem that you solve for people?

KATIE BRUNO, CFP®, CDFA: Financial Peace of mind.

Would you say that talking with a financial planner would give somebody Peace of Mind if they're in recovery mode from a life experience, such as the pandemic, job loss, divorce, or widowhood?

KATIE BRUNO, CFP®, CDFA: Yes, talking to a financial advisor could help give someone financial peace of mind, especially if we just think about this past year. It was an emotional roller coaster. In March 2020, there was a 34% loss on the market. It was quick, and people were scared about their money and their health.

There was not enough information during the pandemic to make sound decisions. Fortunately, the stock market recovered from most of those losses within a few months. In this last market decline, we had a much quicker rebound than we had in the Great Recession.

The Financial Peace of Mind part: sometimes that involves me listening and we talking about life. Last year, I talked a lot about the elections, COVID-19, and other life happenings. When you have a financial plan in place, you can be more prepared. I can use tools, and we can see what would happen if there was another recession or if someone lost their job or had a long-term care event or needs a nursing home. Creating a financial plan prevents you from making emotional decisions based on the markets' day-to-day noise.

It's all about the numbers. We can run scenarios and make sound financial decisions based on those projections. In the end, math wins. Know your numbers, and you can have financial Peace of Mind.

What is the best way to reach you for a consultation?

KATIE BRUNO, CFP®, CDFA: You can call 402.502.9827 or email Katie.Bruno@raymondjames.com

About Katie Bruno, CFP®, CDFA, MIMFA

Katie Bruno is passionate about improving the financial lives of women and empowering them to make smart, thoughtful financial decisions.

She serves a very diverse group of clients and specializes in working with women facing immediate financial decisions as a result of life-changing events. Her process involves meeting clients where they are, figuring out where they want to go, and creating a roadmap to meet their unique needs.

Many clients come to her with financial questions and decisions as a result of losing a spouse, being forced to retire, or going through a divorce. Do they have enough income to support their family? Are they able to retire or are they on track to retire? Is their future protected? What kind of investments and insurance do they have and/or may need?

I believe that everyone deserves guidance from a team of professionals, regardless of the amount of money. The real value of working with a professional is that it helps you live a better life.

Feel free to reach out to me if you or someone you know could benefit from having a conversation with me. I'd be happy to schedule a phone call or meet over a cup of coffee.

PHONE
402.502.9827

WEBSITE
MoreyAndQuinn.com/wealth-partners/katie-bruno

EMAIL
Katie.Bruno@raymondjames.com

LINKEDIN
LinkedIn.com/in/Katie-Bruno-CFP

PERFORMANCE MARTIAL ARTS AND FITNESS (PMAF) – LIFE ENHANCING PERSONAL DEVELOPMENT PROGRAM FOR KIDS

Dan Obusek is a seventh-degree black belt, Grand Master martial arts instructor, and school owner. With 31 years of experience, Dan is a three-time Martial Arts Hall of Fame inductee and sits on the Board of Directors with the USA Martial Arts Hall of Fame. He's an award-winning poet and the author of the book, "Done Being Denied" and created Master Dan Obusek's Mind Academy. He's a father of three, grandfather of five with another on the way!

Conversation with Dan Obusek

Please tell us about Performance Martial Arts and Fitness (PMAF) and how you're helping your students.

Dan Obusek: We have a Performance Martial Arts and Fitness located in Belle Vernon, Pennsylvania. Our Little Dragons program is for children ages four, five and six, and they do a lot of target and focus work. Then we have a TaeKwonDo group for students age seven through adults. I also do private lessons and we have a firearms training program.

Do you work with your school-age students in your school on things like anxiety and discipline?

Dan Obusek: Absolutely. It's not one size fits all– it's a life-changing, life-enhancing personal development program, not just an after-school activity or sport. So, we deal with a lot of those issues, and each child is different.

If you have a student who's a little introverted, or maybe has been bullied at school, how would you work with the parents to get the child up to speed?

Dan Obusek: First, we start them on a trial program. And once they join, before long, they're leading warm up. Two months or three months later, they're leading warm up routines. When you ask them to come up and lead warmup and they think they're just learning how to lead warm up, they're actually learning how to deal with people and practicing being up in front of people. There's a lot of ways to build confidence—like breaking a board. Having that breakthrough—to break a board or lead the warmup routine, changes their self-esteem in a profound way. Then, a couple of years later, they're up in front of a classroom giving a book report or speech with the confidence they learned in martial arts school.

Many kids struggle with the pressure of competition with other kids. You really help the kids focus on their individual growth.

Dan Obusek: Every child is different, and everyone has different needs. Varying ages and belt levels each have specific needs, and we address many of them.

Students earn different colored belts as they progress, but everybody progresses at their own pace. Reaching the next level helps boost their self-esteem.

They must feel the achievement, see the progress, and feel their self-progressing. When they have a small accomplishment, such as earning a new belt, breaking a board, or earning a stripe for their belt or a star for their uniform, it equals one big self-esteem jump. It's a life changing, character building, life enhancing personal development program.

What are the biggest myths out there when it comes to children taking martial arts classes?

Dan Obusek: One of the myths is that kids have too much time and they'll have time to change or learn as they grow up. By the age of four, most kids learn half of everything they'll need to know in life. So, we've started kids as young as three, as long as they're potty trained. It transforms their life into a positive direction of feeling accomplished.

Do you work with kids to improve their attention span and emphasize self-control and concentration? Does that happen in class or over a longer period of time?

Dan Obusek: We teach focus, and anything you focus on, you become good at. I'll take an example, like a magnifying glass. If you have a giant optician's magnifying glass and the sun is shining, and you hold it on a piece of paper while you're moving around, nothing's going to happen. But, if you'd take a tiny magnifying glass from a Cracker Jack box, and the sun's rays are shining, and you hold it on a piece of paper—we know what will happen; it'll catch fire. So, we teach them that focus is vitally important in anything they do. We teach them, "Wherever you are, be there." If you're on the beach, focus on the beach. But, if you're in a martial arts class, focus on the martial arts class.

So, focus is definitely one of the things we work on. We have tiny little focus targets that help with foot and eye coordination, hand and eye coordination, and it's hard to hit if they're not focused on it. And then, we teach them how to parlay that into real life—anything you focus on, you become good at, and anything you want to be good at in life, make it a study. If you want to be healthy, study health. You want to be wealthy, study wealth. And, if you want to be good at martial arts, study martial arts.

What are some techniques you use to help kids relieve excess energy?

Dan Obusek: Physical activity is so important. Our bodies weren't made straight; they're made to bend, lift, pull, tug, push, kick, punch, and block. So, we take their energy and re-channel it toward positive, worthwhile things. You know, I wish they had half their energy most of the time, but we take it and re-channel it to positive, worthwhile things such as working on their form or their self-defense routine or bag work. When I hit the sheets at night, 10 or 20 seconds later, I'm out because I spent myself throughout the day. I always teach students to not hold back and be in the half-baked lukewarm middle. I say, don't hold back. Let it all out and put everything you've got into everything you do.

Can you address some of the fears that parents have with their child starting in a martial arts class?

Dan Obusek: Parents see things on TV, and they think that equals martial arts. They feel it's all violence or fighting. In reality, one of the greatest goals in martial arts is world peace. If we know that we could break a board with our foot or our hand, and we have nothing to prove to anyone, we already know what our abilities are, and we can work towards world peace.

Martial arts is more defensive. A handshake is more powerful than a punch. Make a friend, don't make an enemy. I'd like to be known as the person that helped 20 people, not hurt 20 people. That's what we teach. One of the biggest misconceptions or fears parents have is that their child will become a bully when in fact, it's the total opposite.

Parents may think you're teaching students to fight, but you're teaching the complete opposite—that maybe they can be a friend to the person who is getting bullied or doesn't have someone to sit with in the lunchroom.

Can you share common mistakes that your parents make when they're trying to build up self-esteem in their kids?

Dan Obusek: I teach that there are three types of mistakes. Two are good, and one is not so good. If someone else makes a mistake, but you learn from their mistake, that's a good mistake. If you make a mistake and don't learn from your mistake, that's a big mistake. If you keep making the same mistake over and over, that's not so good. We teach them to not be afraid to fail. Success lies on the far side of failure, which is why there are insurance companies and erasers on pencils. People make mistakes, and you shouldn't, be afraid to make a mistake. Nobody's perfect, but don't keep making the same mistake over and over again..

Can you share an example of how you helped a parent overcome their fears about enrolling their child in class or someone who didn't have much self-esteem when they started, but they're getting better?

Dan Obusek: One of my students who became a black belt is now the second largest landscaper in Florida. Another student and his wife own four karate schools. Yet another one of my students is now fighting and has been on Showtime boxing three times. They all started at the white belt level and we went to the next level and something I said or something I did parlayed them into, "Hey, I can do this and gave them that sense that, if he did it, I can do it too."

Several students were so shy when they came in and now they are leading classes, warmups, and heading fundraising efforts. One of my black belts was in the Martial Arts Hall of Fame at age 15.

What is Master Dan Obusek's Mind Academy? Is that for adults and children?

Dan Obusek: The academy includes children and adults. I get together with local businesses, entrepreneurs, authors, poets, and business owners to share tips and ideas to help each other build up the community. We share business cards, ideas, tips, and formulas. We have different types of professionals, such as the number one realtor in the area and another member who authored 12 books in a year.

What inspired you to become an entrepreneur and a martial arts instructor?

Dan Obusek: It was a lot of small feelings of accomplishment, like breaking a board for the first time or learning how to spin nunchucks or earning a new belt and feeling that sense of accomplishment. I was a C student in school, and I could have done better, but I was ashamed to wear my glasses and couldn't see the chalkboard. If I would've worn my glasses, I probably would've done a lot better in school. When I got older and I was bebopping around in life, I didn't know what I wanted to do. So, I decided to try out martial arts since I wasn't really into team sports. So, I tried it and really liked it. And here we are like 42 years later. I realized that maybe I can turn it into a business and opened one school, then a second school. Actually, I was working a full-time job and running two martial arts schools and had my family life. I look back now, asking how the heck did I do it, but somehow, I did.

Tell me about how your recently published book "Done Being Denied" came to be?.

Dan Obusek: I used capture quotes, snippets, and lessons, and I decided to put them into a journal. Then, I said, "This stuff has changed my life." It changed my life so dramatically that I wanted to share it with others. I believe it took me 10 years to write this book. I believe that every person has at least one book in them.

It's a lot of little lessons, like stumbling blocks and times that I got stuck in my life. Then I came up with an idea and that took me to the next level. And here we are today. So, take good notes and keep a journal. Some of my students at eight, nine, 10 years of age are now journaling. Imagine where that habit will lead them in their lives!

What drives you to get up every day and gives you the passion to help the people that you help?

Dan Obusek: There's an old saying, "When you've been given much, then much is expected of you." I truly am so blessed in so many different ways. Children, grandchildren, businesses, and people have come into my life and through the 26 fundraisers that I've done over the years and helped thousands of people. I want to share with as many people as I can. I don't believe that we're made for everybody, but we are made for somebody, and it might be 10,000 people in your life or 5,000 people to discover them. But I truly believe that we were put on this earth to serve others, not ourselves.

Can you share a lesson that you learned early on that still impacts how you do business today?

Dan Obusek: Even though I'm in the martial arts industry, I'm in the business of giving people a sense of hope, confidence, and security. For example, someone in the photography industry is in the business of capturing others' moments and memories so they have them for years and years to come. So, I think it's a great lesson. It's stuck with me all these years. I'm so blessed, and I've been able to pour so much into so many people. Recently, I had a grandparent who signed up herself, her child, and her grandchild. So, I've taught three generations in one family. I've been doing this a long time!

If any of my students have a business and they're in need, I'll try to find someone else that needs what they offer, like a painter.

I try to go above and beyond just teaching martial arts. I teach about nutrition and how much water your body needs every day. I'm always looking for ways to enhance or add value to people's lives. They may go an entire lifetime never having to defend themselves physically, but they do need that confidence, focus, relationship skills, and leadership skills. We teach those things at Performance Martial Arts and Fitness.

What do you think is the most important question parents should ask themselves as they consider a sport or a martial arts school for their child to attend?

Dan Obusek: Parents sometimes look for an outside source, like a pastor or a martial arts instructor, or a coach or a mentor. They need to ask themselves, "Do I have the skills to teach my child those things?" Sometimes the answer is yes. Sometimes the answer is no. Just having a realization that not everybody has all the skills their child may need to take him or her to that next level or take them to wherever they need to be or want to be in life.

Is there something they should look for if they don't want a more aggressive martial arts school?

Dan Obusek: The school is going to be an extension of the instructor. So, there are some schools that are better at technique and fighting and winning trophies. Where we excel is character building and adding value to people's lives. You definitely want to enroll in a trial program and evaluate the instructor. Ask other parents in the audience how they feel and how it's helped their children. Of course, every child is different, but you'll get some great answers. Also, ask former students. This way, you can get an idea of who's teaching your child because they will definitely have an influence and an impact on your child's life and their future.

If anyone wants to learn more about you and Performance Martial Arts and Fitness, how do they reach you?

Dan Obusek: I can be reached by phone at (412) 758-8352, on my website at http://www.pmafkarate.com, or Performance Martial Arts and Fitness on Facebook.

ABOUT DAN OBUSEK

Master Dan Obusek is the earth shakin', board breakin', mind-expanding and multi-talented Grand Master Dan Obusek, Jack of all trades, Master of One!

Earth Shaking – Because when a GIANT walks, the earth shakes. You feel the earth shake before you even see the GIANT. His presence is felt.

Board Breaking – From his many years of his Martial Arts career.

Mind Expanding – Adding value and wisdom into others with life teachings such as The Master Dan Obusek's Mind Academy Master Mind Group and speaker coordinator for No BS Marketing.

Multi-Talented – Father, Grand Father, Grand Master in Martial Arts, 3x Hall of Fame Inductee, Award Winning Published Poet, Multiple Business Owner, Inventor, and Author.

Jack of All Trades, Master of One – (Martial Arts Master) Soon to be master of many.

Email
tyger20056@hotmail.com

Facebook
Facebook.com/groups/434188811053321